Why would anyone want to reselect a Labour MP?

You may very well be entirely satisfied with your Labour MP, should you be lucky enough to have one. And that's exactly how it should be. Work hard to ensure that she or he is returned to parliament at the next general election, hopefully with an increased majority. Britain needs a radical Labour government that will transform the country permanently for the better.

But if you are reading this, chances are either you are not entirely happy with your Westminster representative's performance, or you know or suspect that your Constituency Labour Party will need to choose a new candidate next time round, for any one of a range of reasons.

Let's consider possible causes for disgruntlement. Perhaps your MP is somewhat slothful, or unduly fond of subsidised House of Commons booze, or a tad too keen on sending racy text messages to teenage dominatrices from lonely Spanish hotel bedrooms, or in the habit of crossing picket lines, or unfortunately addicted to hurling Anglo-Saxon expletives at black women comrades.

Maybe she or he is a former special adviser, parachuted into a safe Labour heartlands seat during a Blair era by-election, without the constituency party having had much of say in the first place. Or maybe your MP is just too detached from the opinions and priorities of the Labour-loyal voters who sent her or him to SW1A 0AA in the first place.

So it needs to be stressed that rank and file Labour Party members do have the right – under the existing rules, as they stand – to seek to put a new candidate in place, through the designedly opaque and little-understood mechanism known as the Trigger Ballot.

Even if you are not looking to pull that trigger, the present Conservative government has plans to reduce the number of UK parliamentary constituencies from 650 to 600, with the Labour heartlands disproportionately impacted. Unsurprisingly, the scheme will redound greatly to Tory advantage. In consequence, the question of selection will arise in cases where boundary changes reduce the number of Westminster vacancies for Labour.

In these circumstances, sitting MPs are entitled to seek nomination in any new constituency in which 40% of her or his current constituents live, which could potentially mean more than one seat. It is perfectly natural that members will have formed opinions of the contenders, and have preferences for one over another.

Then there is also what would, in human resources jargon, be called natural wastage. Each election sees a quota of sitting MPs decide that they do not wish to stand again.

With MPs on average younger than they were in the past, there are fewer retirements on age-related grounds than previously. But payoffs and pensions are generous, and those with substantial service under their belts may decide to call it a day. In addition, some may be disaffected with Labour's direction of travel, or will have received other offers of employment, often lucrative.

Finally, Labour's National Executive Committee has the power to rule that an MP cannot stand again. While such sanctions are rarely invoked, they can apply where MPs are held to have behaved unacceptably. And some of the current crop, irrespective of their ideological outlook, deserve sanction for misconduct.

One way or another, then, dozens of Labour candidacies will be up for grabs, perhaps as soon as next year, and certainly by 2020. This pamphlet has been written to assist party members in making informed choices on this important matter. With the rules written in dense bureaucratese, a plain English statement of what's what will hopefully be of assistance.

Given Labour's current regrettably factionalised state, there is a risk that this offering will immediately be misinterpreted as proffering a factional argument. But this is not a plea for a 'deselect early, deselect often' attitude towards parliamentarians not overly enthusiastic about Corbynism.

I make no bones about being a strong – not uncritical – supporter of the current leadership. But the playing field is absolutely level for unreconstructed Blairites, soft lefts and rampant Corbynistas alike. All strands of Labour's broad church will hopefully find these guidelines of use. And to coin a phrase used by some of the more unlikely MPs who signed Corbyn's nomination papers last year, it's always good to broaden the debate.

Yes, I do favour a return to mandatory reselection, the system that prevailed in the 1980s, which I regard as intrinsically desirable on democratic grounds. After all, that is effectively what Labour's 7,000-plus councillors face, and there is no good reason why it should not apply to Labour MPs as well.

I'm delighted that only a few months ago the policy conference of Unite, one of Britain's major unions, voted overwhelmingly for its restoration. That makes for a real possibility that this issue will move up the left's agenda, and could even be in place in the next year or two.

But that's for the future. Mandatory reselection is not the stated position of Momentum, the Campaign for Labour Party Democracy, the Labour Representation Committee, or Team Corbyn itself. I am not going to be making the case for it here.

You may well be too young to even know what mandatory reselection was, or else need a refresher. So I'm also offering a crash course on controversies over parliamentary selections in the days of yore, by way of an appendix.

Consider this rather a plea from the basic premises of representative democracy. It is highly disingenuous for sitting MPs to come over like a crudely-propositioned Victorian maiden when it is pointed out that they are only Labour candidates because they have secured selection by a Constituency Labour Party. And what a CLP giveth, the Trigger Ballot ensures that it has the right to take away.

The standard counter-argument here is that MPs draw a personal mandate from the voters. There's sometimes some truth in that, although it is never the whole story. But those who forfeit the confidence of Labour Party members in their locality can seek a renewal of that personal mandate as a candidate for another party, or even as an independent.

Finally, the obligatory health warning. Selecting a candidate for a seat that is already Labour, or one that is winnable, is not to be taken lightly. If you are minded to put someone new in place, the only tenable attitude is to think long and hard about the political consequences.

It is by all means within a CLP's gift to take into account an MP's political leanings when making its choice, but they should never be the sole criteria. For a start, Labour does need to increase the Westminster representation of women, black and minority ethnic groups, and the LGBT+ community.

Then there is popularity. As noted a few paragraphs back, some MPs do have a sizeable 'personal vote'. Opting for an unknown, instead, might hurt Labour's prospects to such a degree that the seat is lost to another party. You probably have greater leeway in a safe seat than in a marginal.

You also need to bear in mind the calibre of prospective replacements. There's little point swapping out one underperforming MP for another. With a basic salary of £74,962, lavish expenses and a comfortable lifestyle at stake, many of those seeking a Labour seat could have motivations other than a burning commitment to bringing about the socialist millennium.

But enough by way of preliminaries. What follows will be a brief guide to trigger ballots and tips on securing the success of the person you want to see come out as a Prospective Parliamentary Candidate; some notes on other selection scenarios; some ideas about how selections can be democratised, in line with suggestions made by the Campaign for Labour Party Democracy; and to end with, a recap of how similar controversies played out last time round, written by an erstwhile young activist who watched it happen.

By the way, in case you don't get the reference, the name of this pamphlet is by way of tribute to one of the same name, published in 1981 by CLPD and the Institute for Workers' Control. It was written by *Tribune* editor Chris Mullin, later a Labour MP and junior minister, with help from Vladimir Derer, Victor Schonfield and Charlotte Atkins. Copies can still be ordered via www.spokesmanbooks.com.

A simple guide to Labour selections

Labour's existing rules give sitting MPs numerous advantages if they want to stay put. That's by design. The most recent set of regulations were introduced in the early 1990s, with the express intent of rolling back the democratic advances won by the left in the previous two decades.

Many Labour activists would argue life is now too easy for incumbents, and have proposed reforms that will give the membership a greater say in choosing Labour's Westminster representatives. More on that later.

Let's start by briefly summarising things as they stand. Labour's ruling National Executive Committee is empowered, at a time of its own choosing in the run-up to a general election, to set a timetable for reselections.

Typically, this will last for around eight weeks. Membership is frozen on a given day, known as 'the freeze date'. Those who have been Labour Party members for at least six months prior to this freeze date are eligible to participate in the forthcoming local level selection process.

Where the sitting MP wants to stand again, a process known as the Trigger Ballot commences. This is organised by a nominated officer of the Constituency Labour Party, normally the secretary. It is overseen by paid Labour Party officials from regional office.

Each party branch and forum, affiliated trade union, and affiliated organisation is given a simple yes/no affirmative nomination vote. Each of these votes carries equal weight, no matter if the membership of the party unit in question is just a handful, or runs to hundreds, or even thousands.

Labour Party branches must meet in person to vote, giving at least seven days' notice of their intention to do so. The meetings are provided with statements from both the MP and Labour's Chief Whip, and have 90 minutes in which to discuss the merits and demerits of the MP in question.

This is followed by a secret yes/no ballot of those present, with the decision reached by simple majority. The chair does not have a casting vote. In the event of a tie, the ballot is held again. If it is still tied, then the branch is deemed not to cast an affirmative nomination.

But here's the rub. Affiliates are allowed to draw up their own processes for reaching their decisions. This is where the deck is stacked, usually in favour of a sitting MP, as we shall see.

Where more than half of branches and affiliates provide an affirmative nomination, the MP is readopted as a prospective parliamentary candidate, and that's that. By contrast, a majority against automatic reselection does not mean an MP is deselected by default. While anyone with any sense would probably take the hint, she or he retains the opportunity to take on any other contenders in an open selection contest.

I should mention that there is also some wriggle room here. The rules provide that sitting MPs can appeal to the NEC a decision that does not go their way, although normally they would need to show impropriety to have much chance of success.

All of this might look on the surface like rough and ready democracy. Yet, in practice, the outcome of a Trigger Ballot can often be anything but. This procedure can throw up all sorts of anomalies. Thanks to the equal weighting of party and affiliate units, it is possible for a majority of Labour Party members to support reselection, but for a majority of branches and affiliates to vote against it. Or, of course, vice versa.

Furthermore, the provision for unions and socialist societies to decide their own processes can work against majoritarian outcomes, especially where the initiative comes from head office rather than locally.

The kindest thing to say about union attitudes in such matters is that they vary tremendously. Some unions consult members, others don't, but there is no requirement for them to do so. Officials, either local or national, frequently get to decide on their behalf. For many, supporting an incumbent is the default position.

Moreover, the terms on which Labour-affiliated unions can affiliate local branches to CLPs are famously flexible. If even a single member of a given union branch lives in a constituency, that branch can – if it decides to – sign up to the CLP. If a union wishes, it can affiliate multiple branches to the same CLP, so giving it an outsized say at Trigger Ballot time.

Don't take the word of a lefty on this one. Listen to what Tom Harris, an impeccably Blairite erstwhile MP turned *Daily Telegraph* anti-Corbyn hatchet man in residence, writes on the website of his public affairs company, Third Avenue:

> 'The problem with the Trigger Ballot ... is that it is more than likely that any trade union, with a little bit of organising and a lot of imagination, can contrive to affiliate more branches to a local Constituency Labour Party than the actual party can.
>
> For example, when I went through a rather fraught reselection fight in 2004, my 300 local party members' views were represented by four branches. Amicus, later to become Unite, had seven. The TGWU, also later to become part of Unite, had four, Unison had six and the GMB had six.
>
> That gives a total of 23 union branches versus four party branches, each branch having exactly the same weight. And whereas local party branches had to meet and ... vote to decide whether or not to endorse me (they all did), a single local union official, usually someone who didn't live in the constituency, could take the decision on behalf of all his affiliated branches.'

Harris was reselected, of course. The electorate dispensed with his services last year, as Scotland punished Labour on a grand scale for siding with the Tories over the independence referendum in 2014.

But Harris's underlying point remains valid. At least until now, unions have rarely rocked the boat. If they are solidly behind a favourite son or favourite daughter, that MP can be very difficult to dislodge, even where a majority of Labour Party individual members want to see her or his back.

We will be considering some of the implications of this state of affairs – and what can be done about it – in the next section. Let's just note that some unions, led by Unite, are now promising greater local level involvement. But we have yet to see how this might pan out in practice. For the time being, the main drive for getting a new candidate in place will have to come from CLP activists.

Let's assume that a Trigger Ballot has been lost by an MP. That takes us to a straightforward selection contest. If this were a flow chart, the outcomes of boundary changes, retirements and resignations, and NEC deselections, would also bring us to this point.

You will, of course, know if your constituency decides to hold a selection contest, through your local activity. If you are interested in what is happening in other seats, a list of those currently seeking nominations is published on Labour's official website.

The first step is for a potential candidate to submit a curriculum vitae to the CLP's shortlisting committee. It will usually interview some of the Westminster hopefuls, although nothing in the rules says it has to do that. Its job is simply to 'draw up a shortlist of interested candidates to present to all members of the CLP who are eligible to vote'. In the event of a by-election, shortlisting is a job for the NEC. In the past, this power has often been used to exclude leftwingers, especially those popular with local activists.

There then follows a vote of all eligible individual members, on the basis of an eliminating ballot. This would normally take place at a meeting, although again, that isn't actually stipulated. Thereafter, the successful contender still needs the formal endorsement of the NEC. That's almost always a rubber stamp affair.

So what if you're looking to reselect?

The top priority for the labour movement right now is to secure the election of more Labour MPs at the next general election. We have to avoid infighting where it can at all be avoided. If, and only if, you and many others in your Constituency Labour Party are certain that a change of candidate will help bring that about, read on.

In some circumstances, you may have no choice. For instance, there is at least one Labour MP for whom 'when did you stop beating your wife?' is a fair and pertinent question. There have been other recent cases of MPs whose behaviour is known – at least within Westminster, and presumably to many local members – to be dangerous to themselves and others.

But, because of a determination to minimise publicity in these instances, such MPs have sometimes been reselected on the nod. Arguably, such a decision was not in their best interest, let alone the best interest of the party.

Other considerations about whether to reselect or not have been discussed above. If you do decide to go ahead, the first step is to make sure that you are an individual member of the Labour Party. If you are not already in, sign up at join.labour.org.uk.

Standard membership costs £3.92 a month at the time of writing, with a range of discounts available for the low paid, young people, trade unionists, students and current and former members of the armed forces.

Next, get active in your Constituency Labour Party, and not just at selection time. This is essentially a question of credibility. If you have not been a member for very long, or have not been an active one, a sitting MP's supporters will obviously publicise that fact.

Moreover, it is important to ensure that those serving on the relevant CLP committees and holding constituency-level office back member-led democracy.

If no one else will take a position, step up to the plate yourself. But if you do take on a voluntary role, it is only right that you commit to doing it to the best of your ability. The endeavour will often be time consuming. Such is the nature of activism.

Recruit more members to the Labour Party, and help to build active branches. Labour needs deep roots across Britain if it is to secure change. The bonus for you could be that activists are likely to be more keen on having an activist MP.

As we have seen, the role of affiliated socialist societies and unions is critical at Trigger Ballot time. Where possible, join and become active in affiliated societies and/or affiliated unions. Build alliances with the relevant officials. Seek to become the delegate to your CLP's General Committee, and use your influence to promote your chosen candidate.

More broadly, activists need to win the argument for democratic accountability in trade unions and affiliates. This means taking up cudgels for democracy in union branches across the country now, so that pressure can feed up from the grassroots through to the national level.

Given the centrality of the National Executive Committee in Labour politics, it is important that the NEC includes as many advocates of expanded party democracy as possible. Six of the places are filled by annual ballot of Labour Party members. Each year the centre left Grassroots Alliance stands a slate, as listed here: grassrootslabour.net. Right-wing Labour groups Progress and Labour First also put forward a rival joint slate, and some brave souls stand as independents, with endorsements from neither.

You also need to be talking to other local Labour activists. As a rule of thumb, having more than one challenger to a sitting MP weakens the chance of the challenge being successful. Where possible, it makes sense to agree on a single potential replacement with other dissatisfied members. But if you can't do so to begin with, it's not necessarily fatal.

In some circumstances, having a range of possible candidates might generate increased interest, by appealing to a wider range of the selectorate. If, say, a well-rooted woman trade unionist, a strong feminist, a lesbian activist, and a woman from a sizeable local ethnic minority come forward, it may bolster the hand of forces for change at the Trigger Ballot stage. After that, the membership as a whole will decide on its standard bearer from among the four. It's a tactical call, basically.

Most of the above advice also applies in the event of boundary changes. As soon as it is known which constituencies are going to be merged, try to find out which sitting MPs are eyeing their chances, and work out what to do accordingly.

Remember, no rule limits the size of the shortlist. But regional officials often intervene and try to keep the shortlist as small as possible. Even so, it is often possible to put forward another name.

Finally, those serious about democratising the Labour Party from top to bottom should sign up with the Campaign for Labour Party Democracy, which has pushed this cause consistently since 1973. Join online here: clpd.org.uk.

CLPD has drawn up a resolution on democratising the Trigger Ballot, which is set to appear on the agenda at the 2016 Labour Party conference in Liverpool. It reads as follows:

Full involvement by party branches and branches of affiliated organisations in the selection of Westminster candidates

The Labour Party Rule Book 2016 Chapter 5 Selections, rights and responsibilities of candidates for elected public office, Clause IV Selection of Westminster parliamentary candidates (page 22)

Amendment
Insert new subclause 2 as follows:
'The NEC's procedural rules and guidelines for the selection of candidates for Westminster parliament elections shall include provision for party branches and branches of affiliated organisations to both interview prospective candidates and make nominations to the long list. The drawing up of the final shortlist will give due cognisance to the weight of nominations each candidate receives.'
and renumber existing subclauses (2) onwards to now be subclauses (3) onwards.

Supporting argument
The selection of parliamentary candidates is one of the party's most important tasks. Some MPs serve for 40 years and it is vital that every effort is made to secure the very best candidates. This should mean involving all party members and affiliated members through their branches and seeking to select PPCs who are representative of their communities. Unfortunately, in recent years, the opposite has been happening. Party branches nominate from CVs without interview, affiliated branches are not properly involved at all, and, according to the latest NEC survey, as few as 9% of current Labour MPs have a manual background, whereas 27% are from the Westminster village. The party has made a commitment to giving members a greater role and influence. Nowhere is this more important than in the selection of Labour parliamentary candidates.

APPENDIX

A brief history of
Labour's four-decade selection controversy

Time was when being a Labour MP in a safe seat was tantamount to a job for life. Short of disqualification by virtue of serving a prison sentence or losing the party whip, incumbents were in effect automatically reselected.

Unsurprisingly, this state of affairs rankled with party activists, and achieving some measure of accountability became the principle goal of the Campaign for Labour Party Democracy, a left-wing pressure group founded in 1973.

Thanks to CLPD's efforts, a resolution demanding mandatory reselection appeared on the agenda of the 1974 Labour conference, only to be rejected, with left-wing NEC member Ian Mikardo famously arguing that 'divorce should not be easy'.

Some 12 Constituency Labour Parties tabled resolutions to the same effect in 1975, and 45 in 1976. But they were not heard, under the so-called 'three-year rule' that prevented the same topic being debated for the next two conferences after a resolution is lost.

By 1977, no less than 79 CLPs tabled CLPD-inspired resolutions on mandatory reselection. The NEC urged conference not to press to a vote. Instead, Mikardo promised that the NEC would bring a constitutional amendment the following year that would offer 'automatic reselection in the way and in the sense' the resolutions demanded.

In the event, the NEC fell far short of its promise, instead coming up with the so-called 'Mikardo compromise'. Effectively, this meant that reselection would only occur if a constituency carried a vote of no confidence in its MP.

The following year, 67 CLPs had tabled mandatory reselection resolutions, and on paper, a clear majority of unions were mandated to back this stance. But Hugh Scanlon, leader of the AUEW engineering union, somehow contrived not to vote in accordance with his union's policy. After that, the Mikardo compromise was carried.

Following the 1979 general election – which brought Margaret Thatcher to power – 22 CLPs tabled mandatory reselection resolutions. This they did in the full awareness that they would not be taken, thanks to the three-year rule.

But a more responsive NEC decided to waive the three-year rule in this instance, and to some surprise, the issue was voted upon. Mandatory reselection carried by 4,521,000 votes to 2,356,000 at the 1979 conference.

That still wasn't quite the end of the saga. The Labour Party machine announced there had been drafting errors to the 1978 constitutional amendment, and a tidied up version would have to go to 1980 conference. It did, and it was carried. Finally, mandatory reselection was in the Labour Party rulebook. But not, in the event, for long.

Under the system adopted, the requirement was for MPs to be subject to the reselection process once in the life of every parliament. But this was a matter not for the membership as a whole, but for the General Management Committee of each Constituency Labour Party.

GMCs – the forerunners of today's effectively optional constituency-wide General Committees – were comprised of delegates from ward level branches and affiliated unions and socialist societies, and the Co-op Party. This gave union activists a direct role at local level, to the mutual benefit of party and unions.

The health of GMCs varied from constituency to constituency. In many places, the meetings were lively monthly affairs, typically attended by more than 100 people. By contrast, in areas where local Labour Parties were smaller, meetings tended to be infrequent and sparsely attended.

Where one union was dominant locally, selections often went their way. This was one reason why Labour at that time had more working class MPs than it does now. In other constituencies, the ward delegates had the bigger say, and were sometimes able to secure the replacement of sitting MPs with Bennite candidates.

In still other constituencies, mandatory reselection encouraged MPs of basically a rightist bent to pay lip service to the party's priorities, or in a few dozen cases, to defect to the newly-formed breakaway Social Democratic Party.

After the election defeat of 1983, Neil Kinnock replaced Michael Foot as leader, and in effect built his entire internal strategy on rolling back Bennism, not least in the field of parliamentary selections.

As early as 1984, in what was only his second conference as party leader, he pushed a proposal to exclude trade unionists from votes on the selection of parliamentary candidates. It fell, losing by 900,000 conference votes.

By moving too early, Kinnock actually scuppered his chance of reaching his goal until after the next election. Only in 1989 could he come back for a second bite at the cherry.

Under changes introduced at that year's conference, GMCs retained the right to nominate and shortlist candidates. But the final decision was to be taken on the basis of what was dubbed the electoral college model.

Members got at least 60% of the say, on a one member one vote (OMOV) basis. Unions and affiliates got up to 40%, with the exact proportions variable depending on respective memberships.

The Trigger Ballot mechanism discussed earlier in this pamphlet was introduced in 1990 and was promoted by the right at the time as still, in effect, mandatory reselection by another name. Today, the Trigger Ballot and mandatory reselection are generally presented as counterposed. As we have seen, neither description is entirely accurate.

Originally, incumbents had to secure affirmative nominations from two-thirds of the total number of party branches and affiliates This threshold was subsequently reduced to 50%.

In 1993, John Smith – the Labour leader who replaced Kinnock following another election defeat the previous year – managed to replace the electoral college in favour of full-on one member one vote.

OMOV was sold as a means of empowering the membership, although at the time much of the left opposed it because it diminished union influence. Indeed, much arm-twisting had to be applied before the unions themselves were to sign off on a deal obviously not in their interests.

In achieving what Kinnock had failed to achieve in 1984, Smith had brokered the arrival of the system as it stands today. The task for the Labour left now is to bring about reform, as part of a strategy of democratising Labour from top to bottom.